Nonmonogamy and Teaching

Nonmonogamy and
Teaching

Ashley Speed

THORNAPPLE
PRESS

Nonmonogamy and Teaching
A More Than Two Essentials Guide

Copyright ©2023 by Ashley Speed

Thornapple Press
300 – 722 Cormorant Street
Victoria, BC v8w 1p8 Canada
press@thornapplepress.ca

Thornapple Press is a brand of Talk Science to Me Communications Inc. and the successor to Thorntree Press. Our business offices are located in the traditional, ancestral and unceded territories of the ləkʷəŋən and W̱SÁNEĆ peoples.

Cover and interior design by Jeff Werner
Cover image generated with assistance from WOMBO
Substantive editing by Andrea Zanin
Copy-editing by Heather van der Hoop
Proofreading by Hazel Boydell

Library and Archives Canada Cataloguing in Publication
Title: Nonmonogamy and teaching / Ashley Speed.
Names: Speed, Ashley, author.
Description: Series statement: More than two essentials ; 4
Identifiers: Canadiana (print) 20230443036 | Canadiana (ebook) 20230443087 | ISBN 9781990869198 (softcover) | ISBN 9781990869204 (EPUB)
Subjects: LCSH: Teachers—Family relationships. | LCSH: Non-monogamous relationships.
Classification: LCC LB2832 .S64 2023 | DDC 371.10086/59—dc23

10 9 8 7 6 5 4 3 2 1

Printed in Canada.

To my fellow nonmonogamous teachers:
keep showing up as your whole selves.
You got this.

And to my family, Ryon, Jake
and Noora, who are the whole
reason I'm out in the first place.

Contents

Acknowledgments

Too many people went into the creation of this work, and honestly into me becoming the type of person who would be able to write anything like this in the first place. So here is a brief list, and I'm sorry if I forgot anyone, which I'm sure I did.

Thank you to Eve Rickert and Hazel Boydell for their incomparable support, and to Andrea Zanin and Heather van der Hoop for making this whole thing coherent and readable.

To my coworkers, former and current, who have consistently been supportive of me and my family, making it safe and easy to be out.

Angela and Tarah, that family photo reaction will forever live in infamy.

Danielle, Dan, Janet, Lex and Stacey: you are the platonic loves of my life, and my life would be a lot less of everything good without you in it. You teach me the meaning of friendship every day, and I couldn't have come out, or be out, or do any of this without you.

Andy, Laura and Sid: everyone should be so lucky as to have an international support system in their pocket at all times. Thank you for being mine and for being there through all the messiness and realness. Love you all, for always.

To my parents, who have taken every coming out with grace and love and acceptance, thank you. I love you both.

To Ryon, for being my favourite husband; to Jake, for being my favourite boyfriend. I love you both more than I can ever say. And I probably don't say it enough. Thank you both for supporting me, in a million different ways, through everything. I'm so grateful I get to do life with you both.

And finally, to my daughter—the reason for everything.

Introduction

You're probably reading this book for one of two reasons: either you're a teacher who happens to have more than one romantic partner at a time, or you know such a teacher.

IF IT'S THE FORMER, I HOPE MY experiences can help you to navigate the unique personal and professional challenges that come with being in polyamorous or consensually

nonmonogamous (CNM) relationships
at a time where there is increasing
awareness of their existence, but
also intense scrutiny and significant
prejudice. If it's the latter, I hope I
can assuage some of your concerns,
bust some myths you may have been
exposed to, and give you a window
into the reality of being a teacher who
happens not to be monogamous.

You may also be a teacher with
one or more students who have parents
in nonmonogamous relationships. In
that case, I hope this book will help
equip you to make your classroom
as welcoming and supportive as
possible for these students.

Some of my experiences and
observations may also be applicable
to other professions. As I write
these words, there is a coordinated
political effort in the United States and

Canada to frame any nonheterosexual or nonmonogamous relationship configuration as an inherent threat to children. If you work with children in any capacity, a group of well-funded bigots want to hound you out of your job—at a minimum. This book alone won't protect you from those people, but it may help you and otherwise reasonable people avoid unwittingly promoting their extremist agenda.

With that said, this book reflects my own experience, which is as a Montessori guide teaching preschool and elementary school. I won't tell you how to run your classroom, nor will I provide curriculum that covers my or anyone else's relationships. What I will discuss are the conversations with students, parents and administrators that naturally arise in the course of teaching children professionally, and I'll offer suggestions for how to have the most constructive versions of those conversations.

The Montessori method creates a lot of opportunities for children to ask their teachers personal questions and for those teachers to answer honestly. But whatever method you use and whatever age group you teach, it's a near certainty that your important romantic relationships will come up in conversation at some point. If those relationships happen to be heterosexual and monogamous, they're rarely—if ever—made into an issue. But if those relationships are queer or CNM or both, they are suddenly controversial—as are you. All teachers face increasing scrutiny of their personal lives, and while middle school and high school teachers may encounter less concern, preschool and elementary teachers see the worst of it.

I have been fairly "out" as nonmonogamous for nearly my entire teaching
career. I completed my training to be a
Montessori preschool and kindergarten
teacher the same year I got married—a
marriage that was nonmonogamous
from nearly the very beginning, and
that is still going strong. Early on,
I hid my relationship configuration
from my colleagues and students.
Even while presenting at conferences
from my perspective as a bisexual
woman, I often avoided mentioning
my extramarital partners, because
even people who are accepting of
nonheterosexuality can often be harshly
judgmental about nonmonogamy.

But two years after I became a
lead teacher, I had a daughter, and my
husband and I decided it was too much
to expect a small child to keep her parents' secrets. So I came out, both in my

public life as a teacher and in my private life. I hold enough privilege, and live and teach in a liberal enough and safe enough city, that being out was unlikely to cause me much harm professionally. Suddenly my DMs were full of messages from fellow teachers (as my social media network is primarily made up of people in my profession). More of them than I could have imagined lived lives like mine—with marriages, partners, girlfriends, boyfriends, lovers—and were terrified to be out. Whether they lived in small towns or big cities, their messages had that consistent theme. Teachers are scared to be out about their CNM identities because our very existence in the classroom is politicized, and if we are found to be "immoral"— even in (perhaps especially in) the year 2023—we risk our entire careers.

I have been a publicly out and nonmonogamous teacher, as well as an educator for other teachers, since 2015. And the one thing I am sure of is that there are far more of us out there, keeping it a secret and scared to be out, than I could have imagined. This book is for all the teachers out there living two lives, and for all of the people who want to make sure no teacher is denied the right to work because they're polyamorous and no child is denied educational opportunities because their family is nonmonogamous. We exist, and we deserve representation in education.

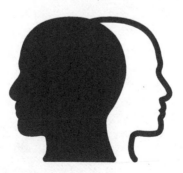

What Is Consensual Nonmonogamy, and Why Does It Matter in the Context of Teaching Kids?

Let's start with the basics. In its simplest terms, consensual nonmonogamy is any relationship where the mutually agreed-upon commitment is not limited to two people who are completely monogamous with one another for the duration of their time together.

UNFORTUNATELY, A LOT OF RELATIONSHIP
configurations are missing key compo-
nents of that definition. Some are not
monogamous because of infidelity, and
others are nonmonogamous by design
but not labeled "nonmonogamy" (such
as casually dating several people without being "exclusive"). For our pur-
poses, we will talk specifically about
romantic relationships that involve
some form of commitment over time
and whose parameters are mutually
defined and agreed upon—in much the
same way as monogamous relationships.
For example, I have two committed
partners: a husband of 11 years and a
boyfriend of just over eight. I have
commitments and agreements with both
partners that are unique to them, which
I do not have with, say, a two-week
fling. That brief fling would not be
significant enough to bring up in my

professional life, or to introduce to my child. This isn't to say that nonmonogamous people should only have committed and long-term relation-  ships, but just as I wouldn't expect to mention every fling or date I had as a monogamous person to my colleagues, I wouldn't feel the need to do so as a nonmonogamous person.

Why does all of this matter? Teachers in normative relationships can casually mention spouses and other long-term partners without causing controversy. No one bats an eye about Mrs. Thompson down the hall telling her students about her wedding to Mr. Thompson, even when Mrs. Thompson actively includes her students in the wedding planning (as many straight teachers do). Ms. David, who has a long-term boyfriend, is also under no burden to hide mundane and age-appropriate facts about her relationship that may come up in conversation. But Ms. Speed has both, which provokes a very different reaction in some people.

Having a family photo on my desk at school that includes my husband, my boyfriend and my child would be considered a danger in many districts across North America. This photo, which I've had in my classroom for years, has no sexual connotations whatsoever. We were at a friend's wedding and so for once, the four of us were in the same space and in coordinating clothes. In the photo, we look like a very normal, lovely family. In fact, before I came out, a staff member at my school once asked if the photo was of me, my husband and my brother. I laughed and said, "No,

it's my boyfriend and my husband."
Thankfully, in this case, the coworker
just looked at me for a solid minute
before saying, "You're a very busy
woman," putting the photo back down
and moving on. In other circumstances,
that photo and my response could have
jeopardized my employment. Looking
at it logically, of course I should be able
to have a family photo without it being
a crisis, because it *isn't* a crisis. With
this colleague, I was reasonably sure
of our amicable working relationship,
so I wasn't overly worried about her
reaction. In another situation, with
another colleague, that may not have
been the case. Of course, there are
those who claim otherwise—and we'll
examine their thinking shortly.

  If a teacher has a partner, it makes
sense that they would share that information with students and colleagues.

This point can be disputed, but the reality is obvious to anyone who has ever taught, had a child in school, or even been a child in school. Teachers take time off to care for sick spouses, mention the professions or cultural practices of significant others, and gently correct students about the proper usage of "Ms." and "Mrs." The reason some people don't realize this happens is because it's so uncontroversial that no one remarks on it. As soon as any deviation from "the norm" occurs, as any queer teacher can tell you, fears about what a child will or will not learn about adult relationships suddenly surface—and any teacher who doesn't fit into the norm is suspect.

Heteronormative relationships are those that align with what we have collectively decided is the norm: two monogamous partners, generally opposite sex. Homonormative relationships have a similar relationship setup, but with same-sex partners. But what is it about *non*heteronormative relationships that scares people so much? I have spent a lot of time thinking about this subject and talking about it with other teachers whose relationships have made them a liability in schools for years, and I've noticed a few common threads.

What Are Parents and Other People Scared Of?

1. THEY ARE CONCERNED THAT THEIR CHILD IS BEING TAUGHT AGE-INAPPROPRIATE THINGS ABOUT SEX.

When it comes to nonheterosexual and nonmonogamous relationships, people suddenly forget that there is a difference between teaching children (even indirectly) about relationship configurations and teaching them about relationship *activities*. We teach children about heteronormative relationships all the time. Every time a teacher mentions their upcoming wedding; every time a child watches a television show featuring a married mother and father; every time we joke that a little boy is going to be a "heartbreaker" and girls will fall over their feet to get him when he's older—all of these situations implicitly and in some cases explicitly teach children about the existence of heteronormative relationships, and we do these things every second of every day without anyone ever announcing that they're harmful to children. Heteronormativity is the default, and it is something we put onto children from the moment they're born, without a second thought. If you don't believe me, you've never seen a baby onesie adorned with the slogan, "Lock up your sons, my daddy has guns." The heteronormative (and violently patriarchal) coding begins at birth.

We usually seem to collectively understand that you can teach children about adult romantic relationships without teaching them about the activities that occur within those relationships. No one seems to be concerned that the heterosexual teacher in a monogamous marriage is talking to her students about the sexual acts she performs with her husband within the bounds of their marriage—because we do not, as a society, define heterosexual and monogamous relationships as being about sex. These relationships are the default, and they are therefore beyond scrutiny. Despite the fact that the vast majority of adult romantic relationships include sexual activity at some level and to some degree, we never presume that a heterosexual, monogamous teacher will indoctrinate their students into sexual hedonism by merely mentioning that they

> Every time we disrupt the idea of what a "normal" family or person looks like, we make it safer for the next person to come out.

have a partner. We usually take it as a given that this teacher is perfectly capable of discussing their life and partner with students without saying anything about sex. But this understanding often falls to bits when the teacher is non-monogamous or nonheterosexual. It's important to recognize these "concerns" for what they really are: pretexts to exclude people who deviate from the accepted norm in one or more ways from jobs, professions and communities.

It is also important to recognize that, as with all identities, there are different layers of marginalization, and queer and nonmonogamous relationships are not interchangeable. In some places, a monogamous same-sex couple may hold more privilege than a nonmonogamous queer couple, because the former couple's homonormative relationship is close enough to the heteronormative ideal to not be overly "scary" to people. A monogamous queer person may be seen as inherently bad by some, but as an example of a nice, safe "good queer" by others. A nonmonogamous queer person may receive extra wrath because they hit both the queer and nonmonogamous notes. While I often refer to both of these identities in the same breath, as I am both queer and nonmonogamous, it is important to reiterate that queerness and nonmonogamy are not the same.

Several years ago, a family looking to enroll at the school I taught at had searched my name online and found an article for which I had been interviewed. In the article, I discussed the importance of representing different family types in classrooms and said that my own daughter never has the chance to see her family in books or classes because her family includes parents who are married and have outside partners. My boyfriend predates the existence of my child—he is as much a part of the family as the rest of us. In this interview, I spoke about how important it is to trust that children can handle the existence of different humans. Children can understand foster parents, stepparents and single parents. It's not a stretch to expect them to understand multiple parents, or parents with a girlfriend, or whatever. Every time we disrupt the idea of what a "normal" family or person looks like, we make it safer for the next person to come out. It was a very boring interview, and I don't believe anything I said was particularly controversial—but the parents emailed our school administration to make sure I wasn't teaching my students anything "inappropriate." Why?

In my experience, the rhetoric directed at nonmonogamous people generally follows established scripts. One mirrors familiar homophobic tropes; it treats any mention of a romantic partnership as equivalent to an explicit description of physical intimacy. This is a crude tactic, but it's also popular and often allowed to pass without challenge. Critics often treat CNM partnerships as synonymous with practices such as swinging or kink—or at least, with the way these practices are depicted in popular culture. (I don't believe that the critics of CNM have a particularly accurate frame of reference for the kink or swinging communities, so in making these comparisons, they often show they have no good understanding of any of them). Sometimes, pop-culture representations of swinging are truly the only frame of reference someone has for thinking about nonmonogamy, but that confusion can also be convenient for people who want to justify their personal distaste through the language of propriety or sober concern.

The second most common framing is to equate consensual nonmonogamy with infidelity. Again, this confusion may be the result of having no other convenient comparison, but more motivated critics often base their objections on the unstated assumption that all nonmonogamous relationships are morally equivalent to infidelity, even if all parties involved are fully informed and participating by choice. For someone new to the concept, and especially for people who have been personally hurt by infidelity, I can understand the difficulty of getting past this comparison. But infidelity isn't hurtful and morally wrong because it subverts monogamy, but rather because it's a violation of someone else's trust. Fidelity is actually a cornerstone of CNM relationships. People consent to a relationship with a given (though unorthodox to some) set of parameters. People can renegotiate those parameters, just as a monogamous couple might renegotiate financial or parental responsibilities, and they can also commit infidelity by violating those parameters without a partner's knowledge or consent. To claim that the mere mention of a nonmonogamous relationship risks teaching children harmful relationship habits, like infidelity, is simply false. The expectations around trust, communication and respect for others are not fundamentally different in CNM relationships compared to monogamous ones. And, not to put too fine a point on it, but the record on *upholding* those values in our overwhelmingly monogamous culture is a mixed bag, to put it mildly.

The idea that a person can have multiple committed romantic relationships simultaneously, with the consent of all involved, is antithetical to the commonly held cultural belief that a single romantic relationship that ends in marriage is the absolute goal in life.

Honestly, some people would rather I simply cheat on my husband than have a whole separate romantic relationship that is of equal importance in my life. It seems that people are more than willing to understand an affair—after all, we obsess over sex and romance in our culture while also being ashamed of them—but the idea that a person can have multiple committed relationships at the same time is offensive to many. Just as queer relationships tend to be seen only through a sexual lens by many heterosexuals, nonmonogamous relationships are often seen as all about sex. It's apparently easier for people to understand the idea that a person would want multiple sexual relationships than that they might desire multiple romantic partnerships.

2. THEY'RE WORRIED THEIR
CHILD WILL BE CONFUSED.

Second on the list of typical concerns is
that discussions of nonmonogamy will
be too confusing for children. People
worry that the idea of having multiple
partners is too much to expect children
to understand. This concern ties in to
something else I see reflected in society
in general: an unwillingness to give
children credit for their ability to accept
difference without fear. Children are far
more accepting and also far more
capable of understanding a wide variety
of family structures than most adults.
When students see my family photo and
ask who is in it, I reply, "My family—
my husband, boyfriend and child." The
standard response is, "OK," and we
move on. Occasionally, a child has
asked a follow-up question, usually

along the lines of, "You have a husband and a boyfriend?" and I respond honestly by saying yes. They say "OK," and we move on. Hearing about my family structure certainly doesn't traumatize them, nor does it confuse them. We see so many different ways to be a family in the world today: single parents by choice, multigenerational homes, stepparents and "bonus parents." We expect children to understand those relationship configurations without much fuss—and generally, they do. So the idea that children can't understand a nonmonogamous relationship configuration is nonsense. It's no more complicated than

> The idea that children can't understand a nonmonogamous relationship configuration is nonsense. It's no more complicated than any other relationship.

any other relationship a child is likely to hear about.

One time I was talking to a friend's child, who was then about 8 years old, and I casually mentioned my boyfriend. This child, who is close to my husband and knows us as a married couple, said, "Wait—what do you mean, your boyfriend? You're married." I had a moment of brief panic, as I wasn't prepared to have that talk that day and it hadn't occurred to me that I would need to. Then I replied, "Well, yes. I am married. I also have a boyfriend. You know how sometimes grown-ups want to do things like spend their life with someone and kiss someone and maybe have kids and be together? Sometimes, a person wants to do all that grown-up relationship stuff with more than one person. I love [my husband] but I also love [my boyfriend], and both of them are important in my life." This child looked at me for a solid 30 seconds, then said, "Grown-ups are weird." When I asked if they had follow-up questions, they rolled their eyes and said, "No, I get it." Far from being traumatized or confused, most children do not actually care. To them, adult relationships are boring, and mine are no different.

I use a simple script for many interactions with children when discussing my own relationship configuration or similar ones: "Many grown-ups want to do things like kiss, or live together, or have children with other grown-ups. Sometimes grown-ups want to do those things with only one other person, and sometimes they want to do them with more than one person. Wouldn't it be boring if we all were the same, or did things the same way? Isn't it great that we have lots of different ways to be?" Most children respond pretty similarly to the child I described above. Adult relationships are often boring to children, no matter how they are configured. In fact, in my experience, children are rarely the ones confused by the idea of multiple partners. Adults are, all the time, but children are not.

3. THEY WANT TO PREVENT THEIR CHILD FROM LEARNING ABOUT DIFFERENCE.

Like anyone, parents are largely parroting the values and assumptions they've absorbed from the culture around them. And that culture has also primed them to be concerned with the quality and nature of their child's education. In extreme cases, this concern crosses into the territory of extreme entitlement to input regarding what and how their child is taught. There are many reasons for this level of entitlement, such as the commercialization of early childhood education and the influence of political extremists (mostly American, but I'm sorry to report that we have them in Canada, too) who advocate for indoctrination via home-schooling. While only a few parents insist on being allowed to "educate" their children with a strict regimen of Holocaust denial pamphlets and physical abuse, their widely promoted rhetoric accusing schools of corrupting children has had far-reaching effects.

Some parents have biases against "alternative" relationships—be they nonmonogamous, queer or other-wise—and feel they should have the right to keep their child from learning about different relationship configura-tions. They believe teachers who are nonmonogamous or queer should keep those "lifestyles" to themselves. These are the parents who call the mere existence of queer teachers indoctrination, and they respond in generally the same way to nonmonogamous relationships, heterosexual or not. Generally, these are the parents who push for the dismissal of those teachers, and they are the ones who demand that curriculums not mention any whiff of an idea of nonheteronormative relationships.

Many of the above concerns are rooted in predominantly white and Christian frameworks, but teaching in a populous coastal city, I have had students and parents from many cultural backgrounds. Some of them have had misgivings about nonmonogamy that have other religious or cultural roots and that must be reckoned with on their own terms. Socially conservative views appear in many cultures, and when the people expressing them are themselves margin- alized in some way, it's vital to respond with appropriate cultural literacy and respect while still pushing back on the policing of teachers' personal lives.

The question for us as educators is, how much control do we allow one set of parents to have over our classrooms? Ultimately, it's a question for the administrators in our schools. Do we allow parents to decide what is and is not acceptable for all of our students? It is ridiculous to suggest that a parent has the right to dictate whether a teacher can mention their partner(s) in casual conversation with their students. If that is the standard a parent desires, they can consider private schools. Many private schools, often religious ones, are willing to uphold the parent's belief that relationships should only look one way, presumably by including specific clauses in teachers' contracts regarding their personal lives. I personally wouldn't teach in one of those schools, and outside of that specific employment situation, I don't believe parents (or administrators) have the right to ask teachers to remain closeted to appease bigoted parents.

Truthfully, I think it ultimately doesn't matter what personal objections parents have regarding their children's teachers' personal lives. It may sound harsh, but at some point, everyone on earth has to deal with the fact that others have different opinions and beliefs. At some point, children have to learn that not everyone believes the same thing that their parents do. We live in a pluralistic society, with people from a variety of backgrounds with a wide range of beliefs and lifestyles. Unless parents are willing to homeschool their children and prevent them from engaging with the outside world, they simply do not get to decide when their children realize that other people exist.

A comparison I can make from my own teaching career is the "death talk." There are certain talks that many parents dread having to give, including the sex talk, the drug talk and the death talk. In my time as a teacher, I have had to give the death talk to classes a dozen times. When a student's close family member has passed away and they've wanted to talk about it—especially when that family member was known to the class—we've had to talk about what death means. When a class pet has died, we've talked about it. This is probably a talk that parents think they'd give themselves, on their own schedule. But there is no "right" time. When the class hamster shuffles off this mortal coil, the death talk is going to happen, whether the parents think it's time or not. And I think that's applicable to this supposed concern— that there is a magical particular age at which children can learn that other humans outside their experience exist. There isn't. Just like they'll learn about death, kids will learn that people are different, in different ways, from preschool onward. It is unreasonable for parents to expect that their child will be protected from the idea that different people exist in the world until an age they determine is acceptable (adulthood, perhaps). If parents want that outcome, sending their children to a school with other people is not the way to go about it.

§

When any of these three concerns are applied to monogamous and heter-onormative relationships, it becomes apparent that they're primarily thinly veiled bigotry. Some people don't want teachers to mention their "deviant" relationships for fear of indoctrinating children. Too confusing, too adult, not the teacher's place—all of these concerns sound ridiculous when we apply the same standards to monogamous (or straight) relationships. This is the point I try to make in conversations online and in person with people who raise these concerns—if these are truly their concerns, then changes must be applied fairly and across the board. I ask people to imagine what that would look like: a female teacher not being allowed to mention that she went to see a new movie with her husband over the weekend? The fact that this is never the case makes it clear that these are not honest concerns. Often, this question makes those on the fence reconsider, because the bias becomes obvious.

How Can We Handle These Objections?

As nonmonogamous teachers, how do we work around these concerns? How do we prove ourselves to families and our administration?

I DON'T KNOW THAT I HAVE A COMPLETE answer, nor do I have a strategy that is easily achievable by one person. It's a cultural problem, similar to the one faced by queer teachers. We need to somehow shift public perception and understanding of nonheteronormative relationships so that their nonsexual dimensions are recognized by default, as is already the case with heteronormative ones. A person in a nonmonogamous relationship deserves to have that relationship accepted in the same way a monogamous marriage or relationship is. Nonmonogamous relationships are no more defined by the sex that happens within them than a monogamous marriage is.

But shifting societal perceptions takes time. In the interim, we still have to navigate everyday existence as individual teachers within the current systems. In my own professional life, I try to respectfully assuage everyone's concerns while holding my ground. I am not in any way trying to teach my students to have the same kinds of relationships I do (also, many of my students are still working on not eating the crayons or hitting one another). I also won't treat the most important relationships in my life as though they are shameful or morally corrupting influences that might endanger my students.

I don't have the luxury of simply dismissing any parent's concerns, no matter how unfounded or seemingly trivial. Parents can and do escalate their grievances to school administrators and air them (often with significant creative license) to other parents. It's important to be able to meet these concerns head-on, respectfully, and to document each conversation. Doing so is professional self-preservation, and it also preserves my time for more important things, like ensuring my school's curriculum meets provincial standards and procuring essential resources for disabled students.

I've been lucky enough to work primarily in situations where my school administration was, if not exactly supportive, indifferent to my relationship configuration, and I'm grateful to currently work in a fully supportive environment. Not everyone has that advantage, so the consequences for coming out or being outed as nonmonogamous can range from workplace toxicity to immediate firing and subsequent professional ostracism. No one can direct you on exactly how to manage your own risk, but it's prudent to give at least some thought to how to navigate conversations with students, colleagues, parents and administrators when they come up.

If you feel you are at significant risk of being outed and facing fallout, or are out but sense a great deal of risk from a manufactured controversy, I think you're probably right.

If you feel you are at significant risk of being outed and facing fallout, or are out but sense a great deal of risk from a manufactured controversy, I think you're probably right. Mitigating that risk takes many forms, none of them fully reliable. One measure is to formulate statements about your family and/or relationships that you're certain you can defend if needed. Using those statements consistently when the topic comes up will reduce the chances of someone being able to plausibly claim that you said something you didn't. For example, if anytime the fact that you have a polyamorous relationship comes up, you simply say yes, I have two partners (three partners, whatever works for your situation) without apologizing or without elaboration, it's harder to claim you have been inappropriate.

Don't apologize for your relationships. Simple, positive statements are hard to argue with. Yes, I have a husband and a boyfriend. There's not much there up for debate. If your school administrator is sympathetic, you may discuss this language with them. Then, if a complaint is raised with them directly, they'll already know what actually happened and what's being inferred, implied or invented.

Open-minded, understanding parents can also be a vital resource in monitoring the rumor mill (parents are much worse gossips than their children, which is saying something). Supportive parents can potentially even push back directly on loaded questions and veiled allegations. As with anything, you only have your own judgment to guide you in terms of who to trust with what information.

Another thing to keep in mind is your personal online security, which is a huge pain but can't be ignored. Teachers have lost jobs when anonymous online activity was linked back to them via doxing. In that situation, it doesn't matter if your political Twitter, sex work from five years ago, or current dating profile were kept completely separate from your life as a teacher. In the current climate, if a third party (such as an organized hate group) broadcasts your private information to your students, administrators and parents, the professional consequences may be dire. It's not enough to be faultlessly and provably responsible in presenting only relevant and age-appropriate information to your students. Anything *not* age-appropriate should be carefully secured so that no one—not even a very motivated Twitter mob—can easily link it to your public identity. Lock down your social media accounts and keep anything that is visible to the public faultless. Don't keep anything on public accounts that you would not be willing to defend in public, should it become necessary. For example, I have a large and public Instagram account that deals with teaching, my life in general, children's books and other random tidbits I feel like posting about. Every once in a while, I go through it to see if there's anything I have changed my mind about, anything I wouldn't want to deal with the fallout from, and I edit my socials to reflect any changes. I also maintain private pages, where I share plenty of info and photos with friends and family that I would not share with 13,000 followers. Keeping those accounts separate is an important aspect of being

a teacher who is also public about
her relationships, sexuality and life.

If You're a Concerned Parent, Colleague or Administrator

If you're a parent who is curious or anxious about your child's nonmonogamous teacher, it is important to reflect on where and how you choose to voice any concerns you have.

WHAT TO YOU MAY SIMPLY BE A CONVERSATION about a subject of mild curiosity or concern may lead to the swift firing of your child's teacher—and potentially also to greater professional and personal effects. Before raising your concerns with anyone other than the teacher in question, it's important to figure out exactly what those concerns are. What specific potential actions are you worried about? Do you have any reason to believe your child's teacher has taken these actions? What ill effects do you believe these actions might cause if they were taken? Do you have specific reasons for believing in this particular set of causes and effects? It may seem overly analytical to look at your concerns in this way, but it's critically important to look at specifics in a situation like this one. Unspecified concerns, if voiced to the wrong people— however inadvertently—can severely impact the teacher's life.

If you are the administrator or colleague of a nonmonogamous teacher, or the parent of a child whose teacher is nonmonogamous, treat them as you would any other teacher. Assume that as professional adults, they know what is and is not appropriate to share with their students. And if you wouldn't question a monogamous teacher (or a straight teacher) for speaking to their students about their marriage or partnership, don't do it to a teacher who lives outside those normative relationship parameters. If we understand that teachers can talk about their monogamous marriages without discussing the sexual activities therein, we can apply that same understanding to nonmonogamous teachers.

If you are an administrator and want to know how to best support a nonmonogamous staff member, create a simple script for any parent complaints related to your staff's

personal lives (nonmonogamous
or otherwise). It doesn't have to be
harsh or rude, just matter-of-fact.
"Interesting—that doesn't sound like it
relates to their professional life. Thank
you for bringing it to my attention"
could work, or something similar.
Simply note that the complaint does
not actually have anything to do with
the standards of the teacher's job, and
move on. You could also direct them to
a parent handbook, if your school has
one, that outlines rules and protocols.
Ask them to specify exactly what
rule they believe is being broken—in
writing, if possible. I like to ask for
things in writing to have a paper trail,
in case things ever go really sideways.
Be straightforward: "I'm sorry to hear
you have concerns. Please let me know
the specifics as per the handbook."
Reaffirm that the concern you have just

heard or read is not actually related to teaching. Reiterate to parents that curriculum is vetted and approved by you, and that your staff members are hired for their expertise and their professionalism. This last strategy is also an easy way to support your staff members without engaging directly with concerns that aren't, as we've discussed above, made in good faith.

As an administrator or colleague, making sure you support your staff is particularly important given the recent campaign by the political right wing (again, mostly in the United States, but sadly in Canada too) to weaponize the term "groomer" against queer people of all descriptions, especially those in teaching professions. This coordinated slander leverages the widespread perception that any expression of a nonheteronormative relationship is explicitly sexual in nature, and that children should not be exposed to humans who exist in such relationships, who are inappropriate and predatory. I'm going to assume that readers of this book don't knowingly subscribe to such beliefs or the coordinated harassment that they tend to inspire. That being said, if you have misgivings about a queer or nonmonogamous person teaching your child—or teaching in general—it's very important to be alert to the possibility that fanatical bigots may try to exploit your personal concern and unfamiliarity with the subject to further their own agenda.

Including Nonmonogamous Family Representation in Classrooms

When discussing polyamorous or nonmonogamous relationships in the classroom, we also need to consider the children who come from nonmonogamous homes.

IF YOU ARE GOING TO MAKE SURE THAT families of different ethnicities, backgrounds and sexual orientations are represented in your classroom spaces, you must also consider different family makeups.

The first thing I do at the beginning of every school year is to send home a survey to all families. It asks questions like, what is the racial/ethnic background of your family? What languages do you speak at home? Who are the significant people in your child's life? This survey helps me get to know my families better, and it allows me to tailor my classroom to my students. It ensures I will take a deeper look at my classroom library to ensure that my students can see themselves represented on those shelves. It helps me see my students as a part of a whole, and that ensures I am seeing the parents as well. These benefits are all so deeply important in terms of building community and building a school space that is safe not only for your students, but for their families.

While it is unlikely that many families, particularly in certain regions, would admit to being nonmonogamous right off the bat, some have said so in the survey. I also like to answer all of these questions myself so the families get to know me at the same time. For the first several years of sending out the survey, I didn't include my own answers. But when I began sharing them, I immediately found that more people were honest and open with me. If you set yourself up as a safe space, you welcome and allow for others to do the same.

If you find yourself with an openly nonmonogamous family at your school, great! The first and main priority for you will be to protect their child from teasing by other students, just as you

would any student
who belongs to a
marginalized group.
Children can be cruel
about difference, and
if a child's family is
public about their

relationships, the child will also likely be
honest about it because they don't know
not to be. This candidness can open
them up to being singled out, and your
role as a teacher—as it would be for any
other student—is to protect them. This
is why fostering a sense of inclusiveness
and community is so important in
school spaces, so that one needn't have
a specific conversation about every form
of discrimination as it happens. If you
put in the work to develop a sense of
community in your classroom, and you
encourage students to develop a sense of
equity and kindness, it is often enough

to remind them that all families are beautiful, that each family is different, and that each family is valuable.

We can bring in these ideas when we start to teach children about different types of relationships. Particularly when we get to the elementary and high school ages, children can become fixated on what relationships are, because they are beginning to develop their own. Friendships blossom and children have to navigate their own social worlds. Doing work around what it means to be a good friend and how that looks gives children a base to consider different kinds of connections with others. When we provide terminology for relationships of all kinds, not just romantic, we give children the means to understand different family configurations.

In fact, using this terminology is an easy way to decenter heteronormativity when teaching older children about relationships. Where I live, children in upper elementary grades (grades 4 through 7) learn about romantic or sexual relationships in sex education. I understand that sex ed varies dramatically based on where in the world you are located, but in my district, these talks are all couched in the language of consent. Educators will say things like, "Grown-ups may have romantic or sexual relationships with other adults, and the most important thing is that all the adults involved consent and agree to participate, in whatever way they're comfortable." By not defaulting to "one romantic relationship" or "one partner," you acknowledge—however subtly—that not all relationships involve only two people. It is important to note that none of this is indoctrination— which is usually the actual fear behind the concerns brought up by parents. By saying things like, "Kissing (or whatever act is being discussed) is something that adults may want to do with each other. As long as everyone consents, it's a totally normal thing to do," you're allowing space for a child to fill in the blanks themselves. It's similar to the way some folks will say, "If you have a partner when you grow up," rather than "When you have a boyfriend." These careful choices in language provide space for children to figure out for themselves what their relationships can look like in the future, rather than dictating how they should look.

So, what to do about families who are not out and public about their relationships? Remember that in many places, it's valid to fear that social services may question your parenting if your relationships are considered "deviant." It is very possible you will have students who come from nonmonogamous families—and you won't always know. Just as with any other hidden marginalization—sexual orientation, religion, whatever—it is the responsibility of the teacher to assume that a child from that community will be in the class and to make sure that the space is safe. Even if you will never know.

A safe space has many qualities, and it often changes based on the child—as it should. To make sure your space is safe even for a child whose family makeup you may not know, there are a couple simple things you can do, like casual mentions of nonmonogamy in a positive light. It can look like a book on a shelf that features a polyamorous family. It is correcting a mean comment about nonmonogamy you overhear on the playground, even if that comment was not directed at any one child or family in particular. By making sure your students know that you are accepting and inclusive of all families, you are showing children who may be hiding their family that you are a safe space, should they need it.

Finally, how do we make sure that polyamorous or nonmonogamous families are represented in our classrooms in positive ways, particularly if we're not polyamorous ourselves? There are a few strategies, many of which are similar to the ways in which we try to represent other minority communities in our classrooms regardless of their presence in our schools or of our own cultural backgrounds.

The first strategy is representation in books. Books are, without a doubt, the easiest way to include different identities, cultures and communities in classroom spaces. Only a few children's books (so far) feature polyamorous or nonmonogamous families, but they do exist, and they are not particularly hard to track down. (A brief list is included at the end of this book to help you get started.) By having these books available in your classroom library, reading them aloud at story time, and including them in regular rotation with your other books, you are sending a message to your students that all family makeups are welcome in your space.

Second, and nearly as easy, is to use different family makeups in your examples, word problems and instructions to students. If you have a persuasive writing assignment, include a prompt such as "Jeremy lives with his three parents, and he's trying to petition them for a pet dog. One parent is worried about the responsibility, one parent is worried about the mess, and the third parent is interested but doesn't want to have to train a puppy. What arguments can Jeremy make to appeal to all three of his parents?"

When talking about different types of families, be sure to include examples with more than two parents. "Some families have one parent. Some have two parents, like two moms. Some families have two bio parents and two stepparents. Some families have grandparents. Some families have three parents, and some have more. Families can look different from each other in so many ways. What do your families look like? What kind of family would you like to have one day, when you're an adult?"

It's fairly simple to change word problems in math to make them more inclusive. Many teachers already do this to ensure women and LGBTQ+ folks are represented, and you can do the same for polyamorous folks. "Nicola lives with her parents, Mary, Ellen and James, and her three siblings, Nancy, Dani and Toby. They share their house with four chickens, two cats and a three-legged dog. Each child also has a pet fish. How many living beings live in Nicola's house?"

If you are a polyamorous teacher, another way to ensure representation in the classroom is to bring in a family photo or simply mention your own family. Teachers often mention their heterosexual and heteronormative relationships to their students—and in many places, homosexual and homonormative relationships are treated in the same manner. Similarly, nonnormative relationships should be able to be shared with students and colleagues as a matter of course. If my husband and I had no outside partners, I would never hesitate for a moment to discuss my family with anyone I work with or teach. The fact that I have another partner does not suddenly make me a threat to my students, their families or society in general. To suggest that this additional person in my life makes me suddenly unable to be a role model, a good teacher or a trustworthy person for children is absurd.

Conclusion

AS FOLKS OFTEN SAY ABOUT QUEER relationships, why must people be open about it? Do whatever you want in private, but why do we need to talk about it? Why must you be so open, so public? Does it matter? And the answer to that last question is, as always, of course it does.

My family, and families that look like mine, exist. We are just as real, just as deserving of recognition, respect and representation as any other family. As someone who holds exceptional amounts of privilege in many ways, who could easily pass as both straight and monogamous forever if I so chose, I feel a responsibility to be out—and loud. Every person who is able to be out makes it a tiny bit safer for the next. In the decade that I've been an openly nonmonogamous teacher, attitudes have already shifted massively in favour of support. It's because of people being out, and stories being told and shared, that the balance has tipped. Ten years ago, I was not out to everyone, nor would I mention my nonmonogamy to new folks in my life until I knew that my revelation would be safe with them. Now, I tell everyone. I don't hide it or pretend my family doesn't exist in its entirety. Perception is shifting constantly, and the more of us are available and safe to be out, the easier it gets.

If you're reading this as a compara-
tive outsider to the world of consensual
nonmonogamy, I hope I've demystified
the subject at least somewhat. And
when it comes to making the world
safer and more welcoming for those
of us in such relationships, I hope
I've made it obvious that most of the
power lies with you. So much of the
taboo around nonmonogamy relies
on soft bigotry, like "concerns,"
"questions" and implications. By
understanding what nonmonogamous
relationships are and what they aren't,
and by refusing to join in a moral panic
based on innuendo, you can interrupt
the patterns that currently result in
closeted lives and derailed careers.

My life's work revolves around
children. I care deeply about education,
about children from all backgrounds
and the ways in which they are treated.

Most teachers I know feel the same. We certainly are not paid enough to be in it for the money. We aren't in it for accolades—we're most often criticized rather than praised, commonly by people who wouldn't last a day in our line of work. I, and most other teachers I know, teach because we believe in the power of children. We are the most eternal of optimists—no one who teaches as a calling can be anything but. I—and all other teachers, no matter their relationship status or configuration—deserve the opportunity to be our whole and complete selves in our teaching practice. When you allow teachers to show up as their authentic selves, you make space for educators to bring their very best selves to the classroom. And all children deserve that.

Children's Books about Nonmonogamous Families

These three picture books all feature polyamorous or nonmonogamous families. There is next to no representation of nonmonogamous families in children's books, and so while I don't necessarily love these books completely and have critiques of each one, they are the best of a very small pool—and representation matters.

And That's Their Family,
by Kailee Coleman

A Color Named Love
by M. Ellery

Super Power Baby Shower
by Tobi Hill-Meyer and Fay Onyx

About the
MORE THAN TWO ESSENTIALS SERIES

More Than Two Essentials is a series of
books by Canadian authors on focused
topics in nonmonogamy. It is curated by
Eve Rickert, author of *More Than Two:
A Practical Guide to Ethical Polyamory*
and *Nonomonogamy and Jealousy*.
Learn more at morethantwo.ca.

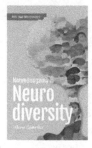

**Nonmonogamy and
Neurodiversity**

**Nonmonogamy and
Jealousy**

**Nonmonogamy and
Happiness**

**Nonmonogamy and
Death**

It's Called Polyamory: Coming Out About Your Nonmonogamous Relationships

Tamara Pincus and Rebecca Hiles, with a foreword by Kendra Holliday

"Doing poly, holding poly space in the world, is hard work, often thankless. Thanks to this wonderful resource, it's now a lot easier."
— Loraine Hutchins, co-editor, *Bi Any Other Name: Bisexual People Speak Out*

Ask Yourself: The Consent Culture Workbook

Kitty Stryker, with a foreword by Wagatwe Wanjuki

"*Ask: Building Consent Culture* editor Kitty Stryker invites readers to delve deeper, with guest experts and personal anecdotes, to manifest a culture of consent in one's own community that starts at the heart."
— Jiz Lee, editor of *Coming Out Like a Porn Star*

Ask Me About Polyamory:
The Best of Kimchi Cuddles

Tikva Wolf, with a foreword by Sophie Labelle

"The warm and open style, and great way of getting complex things across simply, makes it one of the best relationship comics out there."
— Dr. Meg-John Barker, author of *Rewriting the Rules*

Love's Not Color Blind:
Race and Representation
in Polyamorous and Other
Alternative Communities

Kevin A. Patterson, with a foreword by Ruby Bougie Johnson

"Kevin does amazing work both centering the voices of people of color and educating white folks on privilege. His words will positively influence polyamorous communities for years to come."
—Rebecca Hiles, The Frisky Fairy

ASHLEY SPEED IS AN AMI-CERTIFIED
Montessori guide with over a decade
of classroom experience. She has
presented at Montessori conferences
on children's literacy, creating queer-
friendly classroom environments, sex
ed and more. She has designed and
sold inclusive classroom materials since
2016. She spends her spare time cross
stitching, parenting a highly intelligent
and energetic daughter, and sharing her
life with two wonderful men—one of
whom is the world's best husband and
one who writes the world's best bios.